I Know Someone with
Dyslexia

Sue Barraclough

Heinemann Library
Chicago, Illinois

www.heinemannraintree.com
Visit our website to find out more information about Heinemann-Raintree books.

To order:

☎ Phone 888-454-2279

💻 Visit www.heinemannraintree.com to browse our catalog and order online.

Edited by Rebecca Rissman, Daniel Nunn, and Siân Smith
Designed by Joanna Hinton Malivoire
Picture research by Mica Brancic
Originated by Capstone Global Library
Printed in the United States of America by Worzalla Publishing

14 13 12 11 10
10 9 8 7 6 5 4 3 2 1

Library of Congress Cataloging-in-Publication Data
Barraclough, Sue.
  I know someone with dyslexia / Sue Barraclough.
    p. cm. — (Understanding health issues)
  Includes bibliographical references and index.
  ISBN 978-1-4329-4565-7 (hc)
  ISBN 978-1-4329-4581-7 (pb)
  1. Dyslexia—Juvenile literature. I. Title.
  RC394.W6B38 2011
  616.85'53—dc22   2010026581

Acknowledgments

We would like to thank the following for permission to reproduce photographs: Alamy p. 26 (© Ben Molyneux), Capstone Global Library Ltd p. 16 (Richard Hutchings); Corbis pp. 23 (© cultura), 27 top (epa/© Jonathan Brady), 27 bottom (Retna Ltd./Rob Kim/© RD); Getty Images pp. 4 (Photodisc/Yellow Dog Productions), 14 (The Image Bank/Mark Scott); Photolibrary pp. 5 (Blend Images RM/Jose Luis Pelaez Inc), 6 (imagebroker.net/Norbert Michalke), 8 (imagebroker.net/Ulrich Niehoff), 9 (age fotostock/Javier Larrea), 10 (F1 Online/Paul Paul), 11 (Stock4B RF), 13 (Robert Harding Travel/Robert Harding Productions), 20 (age fotostock/Juan Manuel Silva), 24 (age fotostock/Beverly Logan), 25 (81A Productions), 27 middle (Tim Rooke); Science Photo Library p. 17 (Sheila Terry); Shutterstock pp. 15 (Laurence Gough), 18 (Pavzyuk Svitlana), 19 (Rob Marmion), 21 (Alexander V Evstafyev), 22 (Monkey Business Images).

Cover photograph of a girl reading a magazine reproduced with permission of Corbis (Blend Images/© Jose Luis Pelaez, Inc.).

We would like to thank Matthew Siegel, Ashley Wolinski, and Bernadette McLean for their invaluable help in the preparation of this book.

Every effort has been made to contact copyright holders of any material reproduced in this book. Any omissions will be rectified in subsequent printings if notice is given to the publisher.

Contents

Some words are printed in bold, **like this**. You can find out what they mean in the glossary.

Do You Know Someone with Dyslexia?

Someone with dyslexia may be bright, but can have problems with reading or writing. A person with dyslexia may avoid reading in class, but may love talking and telling stories.

Some people with dyslexia can find it hard to read or write.

Reading and writing are skills that many people use all the time.

Some people with dyslexia may find it hard to **concentrate** in class. Sometimes they do not understand what the teacher is saying.

What Is Dyslexia?

Dyslexia is something that affects the way a person thinks and learns. People who have dyslexia can have difficulties with reading, writing, or spelling.

People with dyslexia may find they have to work harder at reading, writing, or spelling than other people.

Dyslexia can mean:

- getting letters the wrong way around, such as reading or writing "d" for "b"

- seeing words as blurry, jumbled, or wrongly spaced

- seeing words as squeezed together or even moving around

- not seeing numbers or letters in the correct order

- confusing the order of letters—for example, reading "was" as "saw"

- swapping letters, such as reading "magazine" as "mazagine."

Someone with dyslexia may find it hard to tell the time or remember phone numbers.

Dyslexia can affect people in other ways, too. A person with dyslexia may find it hard to learn left from right. Someone with dyslexia may struggle to remember the order of things, such as the days of the week or months of the year.

Many people with dyslexia find that they also have different strengths. Some people with dyslexia are very **creative**, or imaginative, or good at solving problems in new ways.

People with dyslexia can sometimes be very good at music or art.

Understunding Dyslexiu

Learning to read and write is difficult to do. The brain needs to sort and store large amounts of information about letter shapes and sounds. Someone with dyslexia may find it very hard to understand how letters and words work.

Someone with dyslexia may find it hard to **sound out** words.

People with dyslexia may find it easier to learn letters if they can touch them and feel their shape.

Many people with dyslexia say that they think in pictures rather than words. This means they can find it hard to understand words that they cannot link to a picture.

What Causes Dyslexia?

No one knows for sure what causes dyslexia. Scientists have found that some parts of the brain that are used for language work in a different way for a person who has dyslexia.

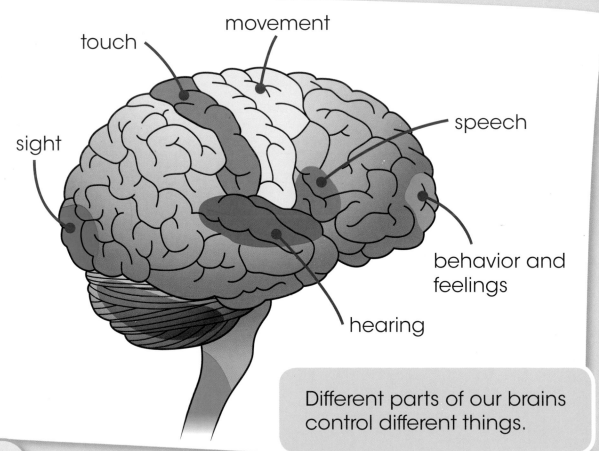

Different parts of our brains control different things.

Some scientists think that dyslexia might be partly **genetic**. This means that it can run in families. So, if a parent has dyslexia, there is more chance that his or her child will have it, too.

Some parents only realize that they have dyslexia when their children are tested.

Living with Dyslexia

Dyslexia is part of who a person is. It does not go away as a person gets older. However, people with dyslexia can find different ways to use their strengths, and to manage their difficulties.

Children with dyslexia can grow up to become very successful adults.

It is important to talk about problems with reading or writing as early as possible. It is more likely that you will get extra support in school, and this will help with schoolwork and tests.

Someone with dyslexia might be given extra time to finish a test.

Things That Can Help

A person with dyslexia may need to find different ways to read and write, or to learn and remember. There are lots of different things that can help with this. Each person needs to find out what works best for him or her.

It can be easier to read words written on the board if you sit near the front of the classroom.

Some people with dyslexia wear **tinted** glasses to help them read.

Some people with dyslexia find it easier to read words on a colored background. Using different-colored glasses or printing words on different-colored paper can help with this.

Using computers often helps people with dyslexia. Some computers can be set up to recognize speech, so a person with dyslexia can record thoughts and ideas without having to spell or write.

Words come up on this computer screen when they are spoken into the microphone.

By trying different ways to learn things, you can find out what works best for you.

Many people with dyslexia find that having extra help in the classroom can be useful. This may be a one-on-one session with the teacher or working with a small group.

How Does It Feel?

People with dyslexia may feel angry or sad that they cannot do certain things well. They might feel **frustrated** that it takes them longer to do things that other people can do quickly.

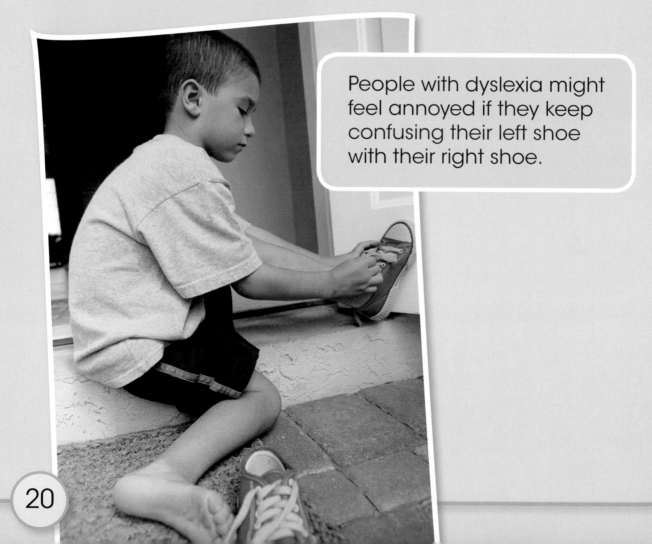

People with dyslexia might feel annoyed if they keep confusing their left shoe with their right shoe.

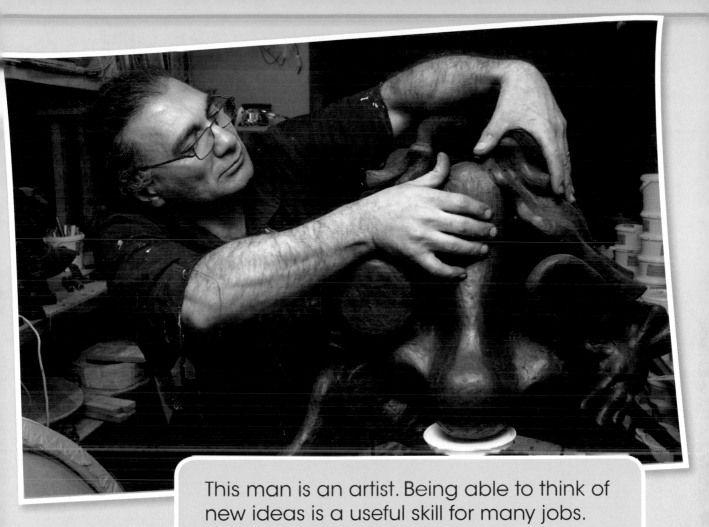

This man is an artist. Being able to think of new ideas is a useful skill for many jobs.

But people with dyslexia often find that they are good at things that other people find difficult. They can often be good at coming up with ideas and finding ways to solve problems.

Being a Good Friend

You can be a good friend to someone with dyslexia by understanding that your friend has difficulty with words. Someone with dyslexia may have problems understanding what is said.

Be patient. If a friend does not understand something, say it again in a different way.

A good friend values the things we do well. If people say something unkind or untrue about a person with dyslexia, try to explain why they are wrong.

How Can I Help?

Some people with dyslexia find it hard to find the right words when speaking. If people with dyslexia feel hurried, they may become more confused. Understand that people with dyslexia may take longer to answer a question.

A friend understands that someone with dyslexia may know the answer, but struggles to say the word.

The more you understand, the more you can do to help.

Dyslexia can run in families, so parents or older brothers and sisters can help younger children to learn. Parents or brothers and sisters with dyslexia can be very helpful because they understand the problem.

Famous People with Dyslexia

Roald Dahl was a world-famous writer who had dyslexia. His story *The Vicar of Nibbleswicke* is about a man with a made-up type of dyslexia. The book was used to raise money for dyslexia **research**.

Many of Roald Dahl's books have been made into movies, such as *Charlie and the Chocolate Factory*.

Many famous people alive today have dyslexia. Others from the past may have had dyslexia, too. Some of these people are shown in the list below.

- Tom Cruise
- Walt Disney
- Leonardo Da Vinci
- Albert Einstein
- Keira Knightley
- Magic Johnson
- Salma Hayek
- Whoopi Goldberg
- Richard Branson

Dyslexia: True or False?

Someone with dyslexia is more likely to be left-handed than someone without dyslexia.

TRUE! However, being left-handed does not mean that you have dyslexia.

There is no such thing as dyslexia. People who cannot read just aren't trying.

FALSE! People with dyslexia are often very bright. They often try very hard, but because their brains work differently they may struggle to learn to read.

Dyslexia is very **rare** and only affects a small number of people.

FALSE! In fact, around 1 in every 10 or 20 people has dyslexia.

People grow out of dyslexia.

FALSE! Dyslexia is a part of who a person is and it does not go away over time. But people with dyslexia can find ways to use their strengths well and cope with any difficulties.

Glossary

concentrate give all your attention to something

creative having the talent and imagination to make new things. This might include a talent for creating art, music, or stories.

frustrated feeling annoyed because you cannot do something, or cannot do it well

genetic something that runs in families and is passed down from parent to child, such as having brown hair or green eyes

rare not happening or occurring very often

research investigate something to find out more information about it

sound out to read a word by saying the sounds the letters make and then putting these sounds together

tinted slightly colored

Find Out More

Books to Read

Doering Tourville, Amanda. *My Friend Has Dyslexia (Friends with Disabilities)*. Mankato, Minn.: Picture Window, 2010.

Edwards, Nicola. *My Friend Has Dyslexia (My Friend)*. Mankato, Minn.: Chrysalis, 2005.

Moore-Mallinos, Jennifer. *It's Called Dyslexia (Live and Learn)*. Hauppauge, N.Y.: Barron's, 2007.

Websites

http://kidshealth.org/kid/health_problems/ learning_problem/dyslexia.html
Visit Kids' Health to learn more about dyslexia.

www.interdys.org
At this website of the International Dyslexia Association you can find lots of information and links about dyslexia.

Index